The Primary Source Library of Famous Explorers™

Ferdinand Magellan

A Primary Source Biography

Lynn Hoogenboom

The Rosen Publishing Group's

PowerKids Press™

PRIMARY SOURCE

New York

For Amelia

Published in 2006 by The Rosen Publishing Group, Inc.
29 East 21st Street, New York, NY 10010

First Edition

Editor: Daryl Heller
Book Design: Albert B. Hanner
Layout Design: Greg Tucker
Photo Researcher: Martin A. Levick

Photo Credits: Cover, p.9 (bottom) Giraudon/Art Resource, N.Y.; p. 5 (top) Library of Congress Print and Photographs Division; p. 5 (bottom) Map by Greg Tucker; p. 6 (top) © R. Sheridan/Ancient Art & Architecture Collection Ltd.; p. 6 (bottom) The Art Archive/Biblioteca Nazionale Marciana Venice/Dagli Orti; pp. 9 (top), 12 (top) The Granger Collection, New York; pp. 10 (top), 19 Mary Evans Picture Library; p. 10 (bottom) Library of Congress Geography and Map Division; p. 12 (bottom) Bibliotheque Nationale, Paris, France/Lauros-Giraudon/Bridgeman Art Library; p. 15 (top) © Getty Images; pp. 15 (bottom), 16 (left) Beinecke Rare Book and Manuscript Library, Yale University; p. 16 (right) © Gianni Dagli Orti/Corbis; p. 21 The Mariners' Museum, Newport News, VA.

Library of Congress Cataloging-in-Publication Data

Hoogenboom, Lynn.
  Ferdinand Magellan : a primary source biography / Lynn Hoogenboom.
    p. cm. — (The primary source library of famous explorers)
  Includes index.
  ISBN 1-4042-3039-4 (library binding)
  1. Magalhães, Fernão de, d. 1521—Juvenile literature. 2. Explorers—Portugal—Biography—Juvenile literature. 3. Voyages around the world—Juvenile literature. I. Title.

  G286.M2H66 2006
  910'.92—dc22

2005002961

Manufactured in the United States of America

Contents

The Early Years

Ferdinand Magellan is famous for only one **voyage**. That voyage, which lasted from 1519 to 1522, was the first voyage around the world. More knowledge about what the world was like came from Magellan's voyage than from any other journey before his.

Most historians think Magellan was born in 1480 in Sabrosa in northern Portugal. His parents came from **noble** families. Magellan's mother was Alda de Mesquita. His father was Rodrigo de Magalhães. He was a sheriff of the port of Aveiro, where boats were loaded and unloaded. When Magellan was about age 12, he became a page for the Portuguese royal family. Pages helped members of the royal court and were trained to do important jobs for the king. At court Magellan learned math, **astronomy**, and **navigation**. He also learned how to be a soldier and sail ships. In 1505, Magellan began serving in Asia as a soldier. He spent eight years helping Portugal set up **trading posts** in Asia.

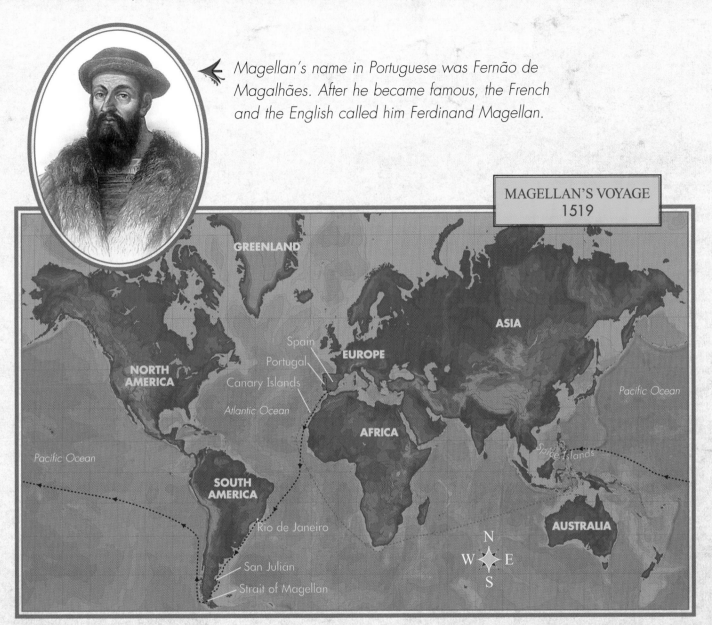

Magellan's name in Portuguese was Fernão de Magalhães. After he became famous, the French and the English called him Ferdinand Magellan.

MAGELLAN'S VOYAGE
1519

GREENLAND

NORTH
AMERICA

ASIA

Spain
EUROPE
Portugal
Canary Islands
Pacific Ocean
Atlantic Ocean

AFRICA

Pacific Ocean

SOUTH
AMERICA

Spice Islands

Rio de Janeiro

AUSTRALIA

N
W ◇ E
S

San Julián
Strait of Magellan

This map shows the path that Ferdinand Magellan took after sailing from Spain on September 20, 1519. After stopping for supplies in the Canary Islands, Magellan sailed across the Atlantic Ocean. His ships reached the coast of modern-day Brazil and then continued south along the South American coast. They crossed what was later known as the Strait of Magellan to reach the Pacific Ocean. After several months Magellan and his men landed in the Spice Islands. Here the map path changes color to blue because Magellan was killed in the Spice Islands. One of Magellan's captains reached Spain on September 6, 1522, completing his leader's voyage around the world.

Merchants are shown trading goods in this picture from the 1500s. During this time different areas of the world became known for producing and trading certain goods. For example, spices came from the Spice Islands in Asia, horses were often raised in Spain, and England was known for raising sheep for their wool.

NUX MOSCHATA DISSECTA,
ut appareat. a. interius putamen durius.
b. Macis.
c. Pericarpium.

10.

2. Nux Moschata integra.
3. Nucleus in duro putamine.
4. Nux integra.
5. Eadem dissecta.
6. Nux Moschata oblonga integra.
7. Eadem dissecta.
8. Opobalsamum.
9. Oleum Nucis Moschata ext.

In Magellan's time spices such as cinnamon, nutmeg, pepper, and cloves were only grown in Asia. They were used to make perfumes and medicines, or drugs. Since there were no refrigerators, cooks also used spices to cover up the taste of food that had rotted. Magellan thought that a shorter sea route to the Spice Islands in Asia would make it easier for Europeans to get spices.

Nutmeg is a spice that comes from a fruit tree. This 1500s drawing shows several views of the nutmeg fruit and seed and a silver grater. A grater scrapes, or rubs, seeds to break them into small pieces.

The King Says No

Ferdinand Magellan returned to Portugal in 1513, as Portugal was preparing for war with the city of Azamor, in Morocco. Magellan served in the war as a soldier. After the war Magellan wanted to become an explorer.

In 1492, Christopher Columbus had become the first European to discover America. After this discovery, explorers tried to find a strait through North America or South America. A strait is a narrow waterway between two pieces of land. They hoped that a strait would give them a shorter **route** to reach southern Asia. Magellan thought he could find a strait in South America. He hoped to sail through the strait in order to reach the Spice Islands, in what is modern-day Indonesia.

Magellan asked Manuel, king of Portugal, three times to allow him to make such a voyage. The king did not like Magellan and said no each time. In 1517, after Manuel's third refusal, Magellan asked if he could offer his services to another king. Manuel agreed.

A New Start

In 1517, Ferdinand Magellan moved to Seville, Spain. Once Magellan was there, he signed papers that made him a Spanish **subject**. A new friend, Diogo Barbosa, who was also from Portugal, arranged a meeting for Magellan with the Casa de Contratación. This group gave the Spanish king advice on which voyages to **support**.

In late 1517, Magellan married Barbosa's daughter Beatriz. The next year he and Beatriz had a son named Rodrigo. In March 1518, Charles I, king of Spain, **authorized** Magellan's voyage to find a strait through South America and to sail on to the Spice Islands.

After Magellan received permission for the voyage, it took him more than a year to get a **fleet** ready to sail. He needed suitable ships, supplies for a long voyage, and dependable sailors. On September 20, 1519, Magellan's fleet of five ships and 264 men began their voyage across the Atlantic Ocean.

 Magellan's fleet of five ships was called the Armada de Molucca. "The Moluccas" is another name for the Spice Islands of Indonesia. Armada is the Spanish word for a group of warships. The fleet gained this name because the goal of Magellan's 1519 expedition was to find a shorter route to the Moluccas.

 Christoph Amberger created this 1500s painting of Charles I, king of Spain. Charles I was 16 years old when he became king of Spain in 1516. Charles I grew up in France. When he first came to Spain to rule alongside his mother, Queen Joanna, he did not speak much Spanish. As king, Charles I supported several voyages to the New World. He hoped the explorers would return to Spain with spices, gold, and silver. These riches could be used to increase Spain's power in Europe.

After Juan de Cartagena's attempt to lead a mutiny and kill Ferdinand Magellan, Magellan had Cartagena placed into stocks. The stocks were instruments made of wood that had holes cut into the frame. Once a person's hands, feet, or head was placed inside, the frame was locked shut. Magellan did not leave Cartagena in the stocks for long. He did, however, take away Cartegena's command of the San Antonio, one of the five ships in Magellan's fleet.

After leaving the Spanish town of Sanlúcar de Barrameda, Magellan's ships headed for the Canary Islands. The Canary Islands are a group of seven islands that are off the northwestern coast of Africa. The islands are colored yellow on this 1570 map. European sailors would often stop at these islands to stock their ships before continuing their trip on the Atlantic Ocean.

Mutiny

Ferdinand Magellan reached the Canary Islands, near Africa, on September 26. Once he was there, he learned that the Portuguese were sending a fleet of ships to stop him. Portugal controlled the only known route around Africa to the Spice Islands and did not want Spain to discover a different route. Magellan also got a message that three of his captains were planning to kill him and take over the **expedition**. The three captains were unhappy that the leader of an important Spanish expedition was Portuguese.

To avoid the Portuguese, Magellan sailed close to the African coast. When he turned west, there was no wind to move the ships. The three captains met with Magellan. One of them, Juan de Cartagena, shouted that he would no longer obey Magellan. Men who were faithful to Magellan rushed into the cabin with their **swords**. Magellan arrested Cartagena for **mutiny**. Soon after the ships got some wind. On December 13, 1519, they landed at Rio de Janeiro on the coast of modern-day Brazil in South America.

This drawing of Ferdinand Magellan's compass was done in the early 1500s. A compass is a tool used by sailors for direction. The compass has a magnetic needle made from an iron-rich stone that points north.

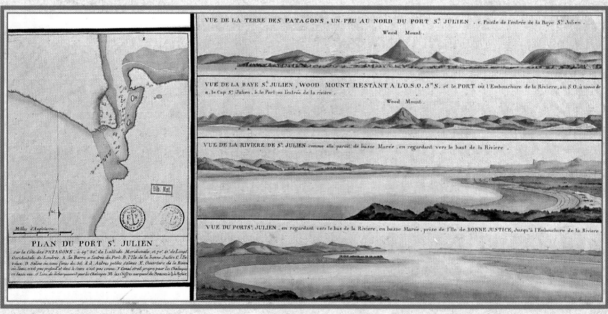

These two views of the port of San Julián, where Magellan and his men stayed for several months in 1520, were done by a French artist in the 1700s. The mountainous areas in the image on the right are the Andes, the long mountain range that runs the length of South America.

More Mutiny

Ferdinand Magellan and his men rested in Rio de Janeiro for two weeks. They traded with the Indians for fresh supplies. On December 27, they sailed south. On March 31, 1520, the ships arrived at a port Magellan named San Julián. He decided they would stay there for the winter, since storms were making it **dangerous** to continue. Many of Magellan's officers wanted to return to Spain. Magellan told them he would rather die than give up. The next day **mutineers** took control of three of the five ships. They told Magellan they would obey him only if he returned to Spain.

Magellan and his trusted followers attacked the mutineers on the three ships, two of whose captains were killed. The third ship gave up without a fight. Magellan and his men spent five months in San Julián fixing the ships and gathering food.

Magellan sent the ship *Santiago* south to look for a strait, but it was **wrecked** in a storm. In August 1520, Magellan and his men continued the expedition.

Strait of Magellan

On October 21, 1520, Ferdinand Magellan finally found a strait. Today it is called the Strait of Magellan. This strait is a narrow waterway between the **continent** of South America and the island of Tierra del Fuego at the southern tip of South America. Magellan did not know that Tierra del Fuego was only an island. In his day everyone thought that South America continued almost to the South Pole. They believed that the only way to get to the ocean on the other side would be through a strait.

The Strait of Magellan is a dangerous place to sail. It is narrow, the currents are strong, and the winds are powerful. While Magellan and his ships were working their way through the strait, there was another mutiny. This one was successful. Mutineers took over the *San Antonio* and sailed back to Spain.

After looking for the missing ship, the three remaining ships sailed on. On November 28, Magellan's three ships reached the Pacific Ocean.

This picture shows Magellan directing his ships through the strait that led to the Pacific Ocean. On both sides of the Strait of Magellan there are glaciers, which are large hills of snow and ice. Some of these glaciers are more than 500 feet (152 m) tall.

Antonio Pigafetta, an Italian, may have made this early 1500s map of the Strait of Magellan. Pigafetta called the strait Streto patagonico. The Spanish named this part of South America Patagonia.

The equator is the imaginary line that divides the northern half of Earth from the southern half. When it is summer north of the equator, it is winter south of the equator. This is because Earth is tilted, or tipped. As the planet moves around the Sun, for half the year the northern part gets more sunlight and has longer days than the southern part.

15

In 1519, Antonio Pigafetta asked to join Magellan on his around-the-world voyage. Magellan agreed and suggested that Pigafetta keep a written diary of the voyage. This is the first page of Pigafetta's diary. The diary was printed in a number of languages. Shown here is a French copy from around 1525.

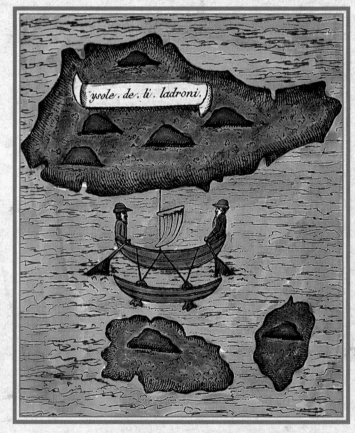

From Chapter One of Antonio Pigafetta's Diary

"When supplies had been purchased and the ships were ready to sail, the captain-general, a wise, good, and honorable man, would not sail without first setting some rules for the voyage, which was the custom on most sea voyages."

Antonio Pigafetta said that when the ships were ready to sail, Magellan told his men that there were some rules that they would need to follow on this voyage.

 Pigafetta's diary is often titled The First Voyage Around the World. *This page, which is from an Italian copy of the diary, shows the Islands of Thieves. Magellan's men called the islands of Guam and Rota by this name after the islanders climbed from their small boats onto the explorer's ships and took their things.*

Across the Pacific

One of Ferdinand Magellan's most important discoveries was how big the Pacific Ocean was. This was a horrible discovery because his ships did not have enough food to get across the ocean safely. "We were three months and twenty days without getting any kind of fresh food," wrote Antonio Pigafetta, a **volunteer** who kept a diary for the entire voyage. "We ate only old **biscuit** that had turned to powder and was **swarming** with worms. . . . It stank strongly of the urine of rats." The men ate leather. Anyone lucky enough to catch a rat for food could sell it. Members of the crew got **scurvy**. At least 11 men died. Finally on March 6, 1521, they saw two islands in the western Pacific. These islands were modern-day Guam and Rota.

When Magellan sailed into a harbor in Guam, small boats surrounded his ship. People from the island jumped from the small boats onto the ship and stole everything they could grab. After fighting off the islanders, Magellan took some supplies and left Guam on March 9.

The Philippines

In March and April 1521, Ferdinand Magellan stopped at some of the Philippine Islands, including Cebu. Humabon, the ruler of Cebu, was so friendly that he agreed to be **baptized** a **Christian**.

During the next few days, hundreds of people were baptized on Cebu and on some nearby islands. On the island of Mactan, however, Humabon's enemy Lapu Lapu refused to become a Christian. Magellan decided to attack Lapu Lapu.

On the morning of April 27, three of Magellan's longboats rowed near the shore of Mactan. Magellan and 60 men jumped out. Lapu Lapu had 1,500 men on the shore. Magellan's men fired their crossbows, but Lapu Lapu's men were too far back for the arrows to hurt them. Magellan was hit in the leg with a poisoned arrow. He told his men to go back to the longboats. Magellan kept on fighting so that his men would have time to escape. Magellan was surrounded, knocked down, and killed.

 Humabon, the ruler of Cebu, was baptized on April 14, 1521. Many of the islanders who chose to be baptized by the Spanish explorers did not understand what the ceremony meant. A ceremony is a special set of actions done on certain occasions.

 The Mactan islanders were angry because the Europeans had come ashore a few weeks earlier and burned their homes. On April 27, Ferdinand Magellan fought the islanders until he died of his many wounds.

A Deadly Trap

After Magellan's death Humabon was in a dangerous position. His enemy Lapu Lapu had **defeated** his friend Magellan. Humabon feared that Lapu Lapu might attack him next. Then Humabon learned that Magellan's men were planning to leave. They were deserting him just when he needed them the most. On May 1, Humabon invited everyone from Magellan's ships to a feast. The 28 men who went to the feast were killed. The men who had remained in the boats sailed away as fast as they could.

Because there were only 110 men left to sail three ships, one of the ships was burned. The men were then divided between the remaining two ships. On November 8, they reached Tidore, one of the Spice Islands. There they loaded the two ships with prized cloves and supplies. However, when they started to leave, the *Trinidad* filled with water. The *Victoria* left by itself to sail west around Africa and back to Spain. After the *Trinidad* was fixed, it sailed east toward the Spanish colonies in Central America.

Timeline

Around 1480: Ferdinand Magellan is born in Portugal.

1505: Magellan serves as a soldier for Portugal in Asia.

1513: Magellan returns to Portugal. He serves as a soldier in Portugal's war with the Moroccan city of Azamor.

1517: Magellan moves to Spain and marries Beatriz Barbosa.

1518: King Charles I of Spain authorizes Magellan's voyage to the Spice Islands.

1519: Magellan leaves Spain with a fleet of five ships. He lands on the coast of South America and travels south.

1520: Magellan discovers the Strait of Magellan and leads his ships through it. He begins to sail across the Pacific Ocean.

1521: After sailing across the Pacific Ocean for three and a half months, Magellan lands in Guam. Then he sails on to the Philippine Islands, where he and others are killed in a battle. The remaining men leave the Philippines and sail on to the Spice Islands.

1522: One of his ships, the *Victoria*, is able to sail around Africa and back to Spain. This is the first ship to travel around the world.

Prima ego velivolis ambivi cursibus Orbem, Magellane novo te duce ducta freto.

▲ This is a 1589 painting of the Victoria, *the only one of Magellan's ships to sail around the world. Even though Magellan did not live through the voyage, Antonio Pigafetta, who returned on the Victoria, did. He printed his diary of the voyage in 1525.*

As the *Trinidad* sailed east toward Central America, it went off course. Finally Captain Gonzalo Gomez de Espinosa turned back. By the time he reached land, 30 of the 53 men had died. The remaining men were too weak to run the ship. Espinosa asked the Portuguese for help. The Portuguese sold most of the men into slavery. Only four of them were ever able to get back to Europe.

Around the World

After leaving the Spice Islands on December 21, 1521, it took the *Victoria* several weeks to sail around the southern tip of Africa. On July 9, it reached the Portuguese-controlled Cape Verde Islands, off the coast of western Africa. By this time the *Victoria* had a bad leak and was filling with water. The men were **exhausted** from **pumping** water out of the ship. Captain Juan Sebastián de Elcano sent 13 men ashore to get supplies. The Portuguese arrested all 13 men and ordered Elcano to give up the ship. Elcano sailed away with only 18 men, who had to work the pumps continually. On September 6, 1522, the *Victoria* entered the Spanish harbor near Seville, completing its journey around the world.

Ferdinand Magellan's voyage took three years. For large parts of it, he was traveling where no Europeans had ever traveled. Magellan died before it was finished, but he established the basic route that explorers would use to cross the Pacific Ocean to travel around the globe.

Glossary

astronomy (uh-STRAH-nuh-mee) The science of the Sun, the Moon, planets, and stars.

authorized (AW-theh-ryzd) Gave permission for, made legal.

baptized (BAP-tyzd) Carried out a special service on someone who has accepted the Christian faith. It is meant to cleanse a person of his or her sins.

biscuit (BIS-ket) A small baked good such as a cracker or a roll.

Christian (KRIS-chun) Someone who follows the teachings of Jesus Christ and the Bible.

continent (KON-teh-nent) One of Earth's seven large landmasses. The continents are Europe, Asia, Africa, North America, South America, and Australia.

dangerous (DAYN-jeh-rus) Able to cause harm.

defeated (dih-FEET-ed) Won against someone in a game or battle.

exhausted (ek-ZAW-sted) Very tired.

expedition (ek-spuh-DIH-shun) A trip for a special purpose.

fleet (FLEET) Many ships under the command of one person.

mutineers (myoo-tin-EERZ) People who disobey the captain on a ship.

mutiny (MYOO-tin-ee) Disobeying a captain's orders.

navigation (na-vuh-GAY-shun) The act of guiding a ship. Also, the act of figuring out the position of a ship and choosing where it should go.

noble (NOH-bul) Belonging to royalty or having a high rank.

pumping (PUMP-ing) Removing liquid from one place and moving it to another. A machine called a pump is often used to do this.

route (ROOT) The path a person takes to get somewhere.

scurvy (SKUR-vee) A sickness in which the teeth fall out from a lack of fruits and vegetables, which have vitamin C in them. This vitamin is needed for healthy gums.

subject (SUB-jikt) A person who is under the rule of another person or of a government.

support (suh-PORT) To provide for by giving money or necessities.

swarming (SWORM-ing) To be filled with a large number of insects, often in motion.

swords (SORDZ) Weapons with long, sharp blades.

trading posts (TRAYD-ing POHSTS) Stores located in far-off areas for the purpose of trade with local people or military.

volunteer (vah-lun-TEER) A person who offers to work for no money.

voyage (VOY-ij) A journey, especially by water.

wrecked (REKD) Destroyed.

Index

Web Sites

Due to the changing nature of Internet links,
PowerKids Press has developed an online list
of Web sites related to the subject of this
book. This site is updated regularly. Please
use this link to access the list.
www.powerkidslinks.com/pslfe/magellan/

Primary Sources

Cover. Ferdinand Magellan (detail). Fresco. 1500s. From the
Sala del Mappamondo. By Antonio Giovanni de Varese. Villa
Farnese, Caprarola, Italy. The Sala del Mappamondo is a
room in the Villa Farnese, a palace in the village of Caprarola,
Italy. Its walls are covered with maps of the world and there are
paintings of explorers over the doors and windows. Marco
Polo, Christopher Columbus, Amerigo Vespucci, and Hernán
Cortés are also pictured in the room. **Page 6. Top.** Merchants
at Market. Woodcut. 1500s. **Page 6. Bottom.** Nutmeg.
1500s. From a medical manuscript. Biblioteca Nazionale
Marciana, Venice, Italy. **Page 10. Bottom.** *Typus Orbis
Terrarvm* (detail). Map. 1570. From *Theatrvm Orbis Terrarvm*
(Latin for "theater of the world"). By Abraham Ortelius. Library of
Congress, Washington, D.C. (map modified by PowerKids
Press). The *Theatrvm Orbis Terrarvm* is considered the first true
atlas. **Page 12. Top.** Magellan's Compass. Early 1500s. From
Antonio Pigafetta's book about Magellan's voyage. **Page 16.
Left.** First page of the first chapter of *Navigation et
descouvrement de la Inde superieure et isles de Malucque*
(French for "navigation and discovery of upper India and the
Spice Islands"). Circa 1525. By Antonio Pigafetta. Beinecke
Rare Book and Manuscript Library, Yale University, New Haven
CT. The Moluccas is another name for the Spice Islands. **Page
16. Right.** "Ysole de li ladroni" (Italian for "islands of the
thieves"). Manuscript illumination. Circa 1519-1522. From *The
First Voyage Around the World.* By Antonio Pigafetta. **Page 21.**
The Victoria (detail). 1589. From *Theatrvm Orbis Terrarvm.*
Published in 1592. By Abraham Ortelius. The Mariners'
Museum, Newport News, VA.